P9-BYZ-273

PRACTICAL POLO

" So, the beginner rides on to the ground to find he is expected to 'stick' to an experienced and better mounted player."

PRACTICAL POLO

by

LT.-GEN. W. G. H. VICKERS, C.B., O.B.E.

Preface by Lord Cowdray

(ILLUSTRATED)

J. A. Allen & Co.

1 LOWER GROSVENOR PLACE,

LONDON, S.W.1

First published 1958 by
J. A. Allen & Co. Ltd.
1 Lower Grosvenor Place
London SW1W 0EL

First published in this Edition 1974
Reprinted 1983
Reprinted 1988

SBN 85131 186 5

Printed and bound in Great Britain
at The Bath Press, Avon

PREFACE

I COMMEND this book to all polo players, old or young. Although it was written in a different scene and for a different generation than the present, practically every sentence is as applicable to English polo today as it was to the environment and time for which it was written some years ago.

The book is full of good sense throughout and any inexperienced player should profit greatly by studying it and, indeed, receive much encouragement from it.

I would not like it to be thought, however, that I agree with every view the author expresses, and in particular I would argue with him about the use of the wooden horse, and in fact I wish that he had put a little more emphasis on the need for the beginner to practise. The lack of time, or inclination, of our post-war players to practise accounts, I believe, for the fact that so few of them are improving sufficiently to take the place of the old hands.

Finally, I would like to say how glad I am that the book is to be republished, for it can do nothing but good to those who read it, whether it be to teach the young player what to do or the old player what not to do.

COWDRAY

CONTENTS

ILLUSTRATIONS

FOREWORD

MANY books have been written on polo, but none, so far as I know, give much of that elementary and personal information which is so wanted by the beginner and so helpful to others who have not studied the game very deeply.

In this book I have attempted to give practical hints for the player of club polo. Those who have attained the standard of first class polo tournaments will not only not require the advice given herein, but perhaps will differ with much that is written. This is only to be expected, for there are many interpretations of the king of games—Polo.

No mention is made of the choosing and training of polo ponies. This subject requires a book to itself, and, indeed, several have been written.

Many men play polo for years without, apparently, giving much thought to details and do not perceive that they are committing small tactical crimes which mitigate against their prowess and enjoyment. The pace, excitement and preoccupation of riding prevent a great number of players appreciating the niceties of the game.

In this book I have given information which many

players cannot obtain because they have no one to ask. It contains much that is extremely elementary but will have attained its object if it enables a few to improve their game.

W. G. H. VICKERS

Chapter I

TIPS FOR THE BEGINNER

IN no game does a beginner start to play with so many disadvantages and so many perplexities as in polo. He will have to learn, as a rule, on an inferior pony, for no one will take the risk of having a good one spoilt by a novice and few beginners can afford to acquire knowledge of polo on a prefectly-trained and therefore expensive animal.

The tiro probably begins to learn the most difficult of all games handicapped by a mount which is not easy to ride and which possibly will engage all his attention. There is in this no reflection on his riding because polo requires horsemanship of a kind which can only be acquired by experience and practice. A man may be first class in the hunting field and yet not have the particular balance and knowledge of the aids which are required in polo. The polo ground is the best of riding schools and the beginner, even if he has not much previous experience, will soon find himself improving. He will, however, do well to start the game on a quiet animal and, above all, on one which does not pull.

Length of Stirrups

Every man's seat on a horse varies according to his height and shape but he should remember that his prowess at polo may be affected by the length of his stirrups.

An American once said, " If you want to hit a thing you don't sit down to do it."

Polo is the only game in which one does not stand when striking the ball! The man who rides short, in a sitting position like a jockey, will find that the attitude makes it hard for him to move in such a way as to hit freely many of the shots necessary in play; and, moreover, it will be more difficult for him, if riding short, to compensate while in the act of striking for the up and down motion of the pony.

If the beginner will notice the length of stirrups of, say, ten first class players, he will see that the majority ride long rather than short. Enquiry will probably elicit also the fact that they ride with longer stirrups when playing polo than at other times.

It is generally easier to control a difficult pony when riding short and the rider will consider this, but he is recommended, if he would improve his accuracy and distance in hitting, to lengthen his stirrups as much as he can with security and comfort. He may find it awkward at first to ride thus, but his improved hitting will soon more than compensate for any initial discomfort he may feel.

Polo Tactics

To few beginners are the details and tactics of the game explained before they venture to take part in club polo. Having spent a few hours practising with stick and ball the novice is probably ushered on to the field with some such remark as:—

" Don't worry. Stick to your man and listen for my directions. I'll tell you what to do but mind you don't cross."

So he rides on to the ground to find that he is expected to " stick " to an experienced and better mounted player to whom he fails utterly to adhere; the rushing of the wind in his ears effectually drowns the sound of any instructions; and, as for crossing, not only is he somewhat hazy as to its exact meaning but his pony engages so much of his attention that he cannot attend to such a detail.

That, for the beginner, is POLO. At the end of a few weeks' play he can keep himself and his pony out of danger; can make spasmodic dives at the ball; and has perhaps learnt to get angry when shouted at. He gets, however, much strenuous exercise, his liver is shaken up, and he acquires an excellent thirst; all of which fortifies him in his opinion that there is no game like polo. Having arrived at this stage there is the probability that unless called upon to play in a team in some tournament he will not give much thought to the improvement of his game.

This prospect of mediocrity can be averted by being taken in hand by an experienced player; but few are fortunate enough to acquire a sufficiently painstaking tutor. The alternative (which the succeeding chapters of this book attempt to provide) is for him to read up the duties of the various players in a side so that on taking the field he has a good idea of what is expected of him and how he should endeavour to pull his weight.

The rules of polo, the fouls and penalties, are given in the *Polo Calendar*, but without some knowledge of the game they are difficult to understand and few beginners trouble to study them. They would do well to spend half an hour running through the rules with an old player who can explain the intricacies of the various fouls.

It is customary to request the beginner to play No. 1 (a difficult position) because, presumably, he will be less in the way or will do least harm in that place! Of this matter more will be said later, but since No. 1 is the position in which almost certainly he will have to make his debut, the beginning of Chapter III should be carefully studied by the novice.

Riding Off

The order which will be shouted (or perhaps screamed!) at him most often will be: " Ride your man."

So easy to say—so difficult to do; and, oddly enough,

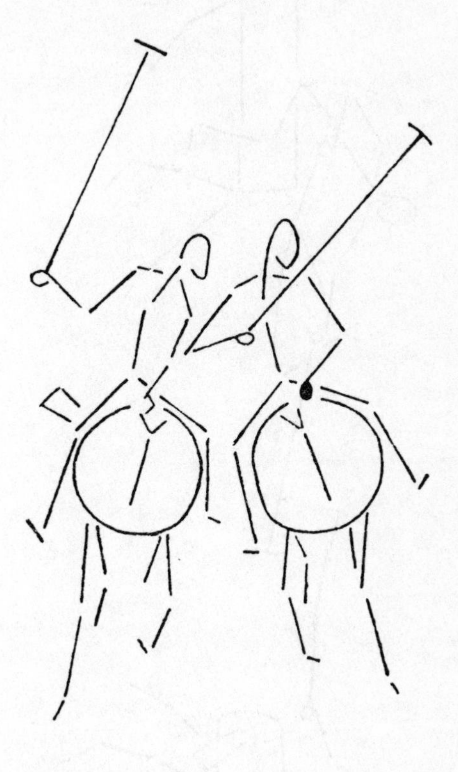

Using the elbow when riding off—a foul!

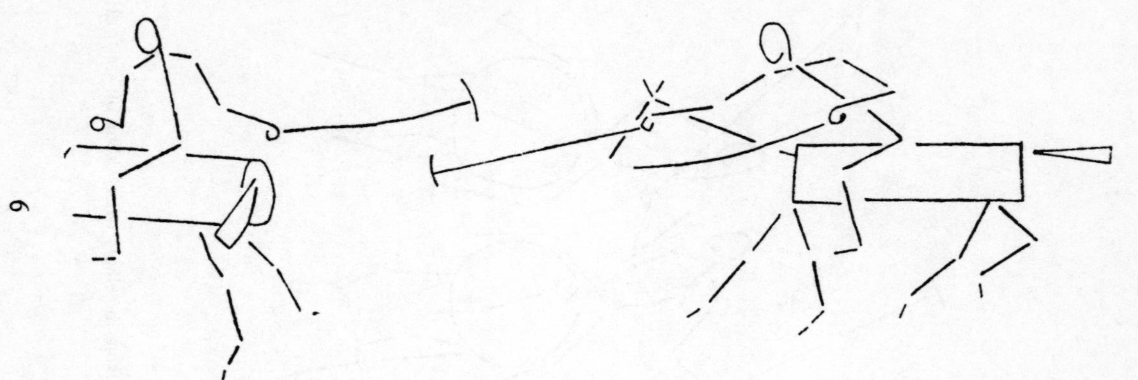

That desperate effort to hook his stick.

this order is generally heard by the No. 1 when he has already tried and *failed* to ride his man!

In the business of riding off, more perhaps than in any other, does experience have most weight. The old player always seems to have the advantage of the beginner and try how he may the latter will seldom prevent him reaching the ball. No amount of reading will teach a man how to ride off, but a few elementary tips may help.

If he has any choice in the matter he should always try to ride his man on the latter's " off " side (that is, his stick side). In so doing he not only prevents his opponent using his stick on the easier (off) side but he himself has his stick arm free to hit the ball. An experienced player will instinctively avoid being ridden on his right side and will endeavour to attack his opponent on that side.

The ideal position in which to be when riding the man is with the knee against the horse's shoulder and immediately in front of his knee. The opponent will then be at the disadvantage either of having to give way or of riding " through " the obstructing knee in order to pass ahead.

It is obvious that to obtain the above advantage of position it is desirable not only to get in a bump before he is ready (difficult to do when taking on an old hand!) but also to be in a good position before the bump takes place. This desirable position is about a neck (or say three feet) ahead of the opponent.

A well trained pony can throw his weight in and ride off on whichever leg he happens to be galloping, but he can do so with most effect when galloping on the leg nearer to his opponent. In other words, if he is riding off an adversary on his left it is better that he should be galloping on the near fore. If he happens, in such a case, to be on the off fore he will be at a disadvantage. It has been said that an old pony will change on to the correct leg of his own accord, but this is not a common trait. This point is really only of theoretical interest because few horsemen in the heat of the game will be able to aid his pony on to the most favourable leg. Nevertheless, failure to ride off the man successfully may often be attributed to this fact.

Marking the Man

When marking his man, any but an experienced player should ride close to (say within two yards of) him. It is a mistake to think that a man may be marked by riding a horse's length or more ahead, or by keeping some distance between him and the ball in play. A good player so inadequately marked will, without difficulty, give his opponent the slip; particularly if the latter has his back turned.

So let the beginner ride next to his man (if possible on his off side) and with his pony's head about three feet in front. In this position not only will he have the best chance of doing his job but he will probably so embarrass his opponent as to put him off his game. Nothing is so irritating as to feel the perpetual necessity of having to shake off an adversary before one can have free access to the ball.

By marking his man well a player who may be an indifferent hitter will pull his weight in the best company.

One more point on the subject of riding off may be mentioned here. A player will frequently find that his particular man, whom it is his duty to mark, has given him the slip and cannot be caught. It is generally inadvisable to chase after him and far better to ride off another member of the opposing team who is near by until such time that his own particular man comes again within reach.

The beginner may take it as a sound maxim that " *to be riding no one is to be doing wrong*."

Turning Up

Another familiar shout on the polo field is " Turn." This is generally shouted when a backhander is about to be hit, say, by one of the defending backs. Sometimes the position of the striker will give the clue as to the direction in which the ball will be hit, and the other members of the side will turn up in that direction. It very often occurs, however, that the striker's position gives no such indication. In these circumstances the following general rule is strongly recommended to the novice, at least until he has reason to follow another method.

If the ball is in the defender's half of the ground—Turn outwards (i.e., towards the touch line), because the striker will almost invariably try to clear the ball away from the goal mouth towards the wing.

If the ball is in the adversary's half of the ground—Turn inwards towards the centre of the field, because the striker will generally drive the ball in the direction of the enemy's goal.

Hitting The Ball

Hitting the ball is a matter of practice, a subject dealt with in Chapter II, but a few words may be said here because marking the man, riding off and turning are liable to pall after a time and a beginner naturally desires above everything to imitate those long shots which some players seem to make with such ease.

Correct style in hitting a polo ball is as valuable as in any other game, and yet few beginners give much thought to this point. Style can only be taught by practical demonstration but two small points can be referred to here.

The first is, that although the arm and the wrist are kept flexible during the swing, at the actual moment of impact the arm should be absolutely straight. It will be noticed that no first class player hits the ball with a bent elbow (save in exceptional circumstances such as in a mêlée or on a very bumpy ground).

The second point is that when making a forward shot the weight of the body should be taken as much as possible on the thighs. This position enables the striker to compensate for the motion of the horse and allows him to hit with a strength impossible when sitting back on the seat of the saddle.

In all ball games the secret of long hitting is in the " timing " and not in the amount of strength applied, but in polo, of course, the faster the pace the greater the wind resistance to the stick and this entails slightly greater effort in striking.

Polo Sense

" Keep your eye on the ball " is a precept common to all ball games but it is usually understood to apply when actually striking at the ball. In polo more than this is required and one might well change the sentence to read " Keep your eye on the game "!

Some players have what is called " polo sense " which may be defined as the sense of anticipation. No man who fails to watch continually the movements of the ball and the positions of other players can possibly anticipate the movements of the game. Some men have the uncanny knack of being always in the right place and of foreseeing the position of the ball. These men it will be observed, even when " riding off " their man, generally twist in the saddle in such a way as to be able to watch the ball even when it is behind them.

There are times, of course, when it is quite impossible to watch the ball, but the experienced player reduces these to a minimum. A man who, owing to his inflexibility in the saddle or for any other reason, can look only to his front will never be a good performer and will, moreover, be a danger to his fellow players.

Polo—A Fore and Aft Game

Polo, unlike football or hockey, is a game which disposes itself " fore and aft." There is no right wing or left wing player, and in good polo one seldom sees two members of the same side level with each other. There are certain occasions in a well trained team that players will so ride, but in club polo generally and for the beginner in particular the effort should be made either to get ahead of the striker or to drop behind him so as to back him up. The comparative pace of the ponies will indicate whether to drop back or not, but as a rule a No. 1 will endeavour to get ahead of his No. 2 and the latter ahead of his No. 3, so that their relative positions in the team may not be altered.

In using the word " ahead " the beginner should note that straight ahead, i.e., between the striker and the opposing goal, is meant.

Backing Up

Backing up a member of the same side often presents difficulties. The object in backing up is to be in position to hit the ball if the man in front misses it; and to do this easily it is desirable to follow some considerable distance behind so as to get a clear view of the ball and time to prepare for the shot. Unfortunately, there will also be a member of the opposing side equally interested in the matter, and he may forge ahead to get at the ball first. It is obviously undesirable that he should do this but, on the other hand, it is useless to ride on the tail of the player in front because there will be no time to see or

Riding through the goal mouth. Odds against a goal!

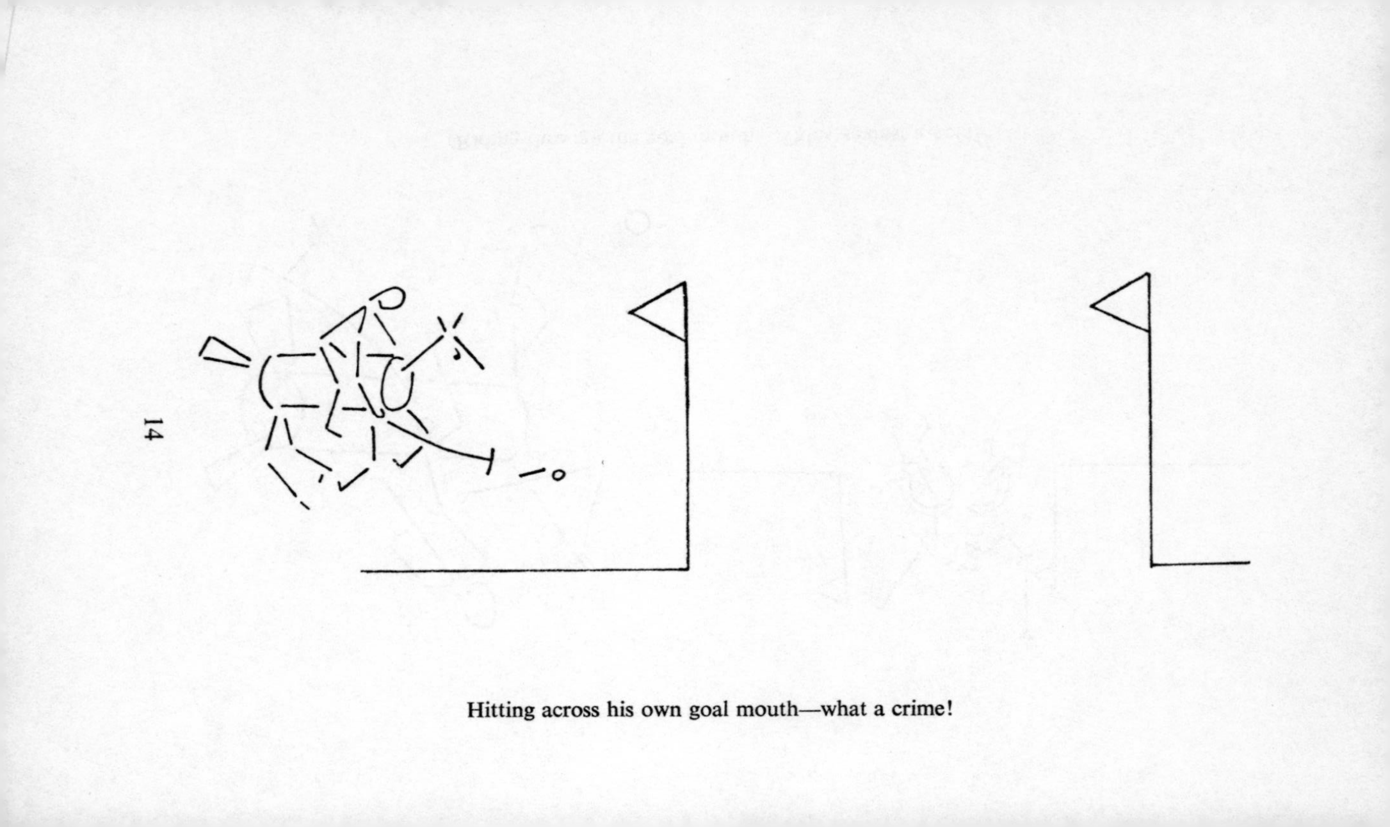

Hitting across his own goal mouth—what a crime!

strike the ball if he should miss it. A good normal distance to keep when backing up is twenty yards which, if pressed by an opponent, may be reduced to fifteen but it is considered that no useful purpose is served in going up closer than this.

Leaving the Ball

Orders on the polo field should be obeyed without question. If they are wrongly given, the discussion on the subject should be postponed to that calmer atmosphere which prevails in the club house or round the drink table. Unfortunately there are in all clubs certain selfish players whose sole object is to hit the ball as often as possible without regard to the tactics of the game. Nevertheless, all players should give the man in the rear the credit of having a good reason for shouting instructions and should obey at once.

Beginners, sometimes from fright and sometimes from modesty, leave to someone behind, a ball which they themselves could and should hit. There are, of course, certain occasions when this should be done—occasions which will be recognized by experienced players and in well drilled teams—but in club polo there are few occasions on which the man in rear should shout " Leave it " (or " Go ").

The beginner is advised always to hit the ball if it is before him and he is on the line of it unless he is definitely told not to do so.

As will be explained in a subsequent chapter the duty of

the No. 3 and back is to send the ball up to the No. 1 and No. 2. If, therefore, one of these forwards finds the ball ahead of him, he should assume that it was sent there for him to *hit*, not to leave.

Clearing the Goal Mouth

Few things are more annoying than to make a good shot at goal only to see the ball strike the pony of a player in front. It is a common fault with many players —not only beginners!—to ride ahead of the man in possession of the ball straight through the goal mouth (*see* page 13). By so doing they very frequently prevent a goal being scored. The object should be to clear the goal mouth as soon as the man in possession of the ball is within shooting distance, and every effort must be made not only to keep out of the way oneself but also to ride the opposing player away from the goal mouth.

Hitting Across the Goal Mouth

A player, even if his place is forward (i.e., No. 1 or No. 2), will often find himself in the position to make a defensive shot in the vicinity of his own goal, when a back-hander (or perhaps a forward shot) will be necessary. He should avoid hitting the ball *across the mouth* of his own goal. Good players will occasionally do so but the risk is very great and they do it with the knowledge of the risk that they are taking, and that if they mishit, a goal will most likely be scored against them.

This risky shot is usually made by a player who either

has lost his head in the excitement of the game or has a limited knowledge of polo.

The only occasion on which a shot across the goal mouth in defence is justified is when by so doing the player converts a very dangerous situation into a strong attack.

Hooking Sticks

It is surprising that beginners so very seldom make an attempt to hook an adversary's stick when the latter is striking at the ball. So long as he is on the same side of his opponent as is the ball, he may hook his stick and should do so.

Many players seem to think that hooking a stick is an unsportsmanlike act. There is no doubt that to have one's stick hooked is most exasperating but it is quite fair and should be expected. Many young players who have failed to catch or ride off a man can still do their job by attempting to hook his stick. This is best done by striking gently at the opponent's stick as it is about to hit the ball; this is more effective than to merely place the stick in the way.

Bad Example

Many players are led into playing bad polo by the bad example set them by older players. The latter in club polo often take risks and foul in a manner which would be impossible in a tournament.

Many of them will urge the beginner to " ride the

man " and at the same time omit to fulfil their own obligations in that respect!

Others, exasperated by the incapacity of members of their own side, will disregard correct tactics and leaving their place will play a selfish or otherwise incorrect game.

In concluding this chapter it is well to warn the beginner that club polo may be watched with advantage only if done so in a critical spirit. It is prolific in examples of bad tactics and wrong play, and if he would learn the game by watching he should confine himself to good tournament polo.

Chapter II

ON HITTING THE BALL AND HOW TO PRACTISE

IT is a remarkable fact that few polo players give much thought to, or even practise, extreme *accuracy* in hitting the ball. Rough and ready methods and a comparatively low standard are cheerfully accepted.

Clean and accurate hitting is as necessary in polo as in any other game, but it requires practice—*practice on the right lines*. A man is unlikely to become a first class player if he relies for practice on club games alone. Polo is a hard task mistress and in the early stages the aspiring novice may find that there is little time for other games.

The owner of as few as two ponies can get as much practice as he needs because, fortunately, the mentality of the average horse is such that repetition does not bore him or make him (mentally) stale. (A horse will become physically stale, of course, with too much work and need rest and change.) The player can rely on two or more days a week (other than polo days) on which to practise without harming his ponies. So long as practice does not, through ill-treatment or unsoundness, entail pain few ponies object to long periods of hitting the ball about. Indeed the majority, including old ponies, are improved by it. It is a fallacy to suppose that ponies invariably need absolute rest between polo days; half an hour of practice at a slow pace on off days will not harm a fit animal.

Choice of Sticks

Before discussing practice in hitting the ball a word must be said on the choice of polo sticks.

Most players do not give as much care to the selection of polo sticks as they would to choosing a cricket bat or golf club. This is probably because the points to be looked for in a polo stick are not generally known.

The length of sticks used nowadays varies from fifty to fifty-six inches. Few will disagree with the statement that the shorter the stick used the better is the control of it and consequently the greater the accuracy in hitting. Players are recommended, therefore, to use the shortest stick they can wield in comfort. Slim lithe men who are good horsemen will be able to use shorter sticks than those who, owing to their configuration or rigidity in the saddle, are unable to bend about very much.

The beginner is recommended to start playing with a comparatively long stick (say, 54 inches) so as to avoid acquiring that distressing habit of "diving" or "digging" at the ball. As he becomes proficient he can gradually use sticks of less length.

It may be urged that the length of stick will vary with the height of the pony.

This is a controversial point!

Many players consider that (within reasonable limits) the same length stick should be used on all ponies. They argue that the balance varies considerably between sticks of different length and this is a disadvantage. They also point out that a player, if he would be an accurate hitter, must know instinctively the exact distance from his hand of the head of the stick and will compensate for the distance of the ball from his eye by bending, just as he does at tennis or hockey. If the distance of the head of the stick from his hand varies it makes accurate hitting more difficult.

Others will not agree and will use a different length of stick for each pony. In this case it should be remembered that it is the actual height of the rider from the ground which rules the length of the stick and not the official (withers) measurement of the pony. Two ponies of different wither measurement may carry a rider the same distance from the ground. Then, again, some ponies gallop " nearer to the ground " than others, of similar measurement.

The flexibility of the cane is of great importance; and the reason for this is sometimes not understood. Accurate hitting requires exact timing. Timing varies with the pliancy of the stick. The timing, using a whippy stick, differs from that with a stiff one because wind resistance tends to hold back the stick head. In the case of the whippy stick the head is left behind and follows after the

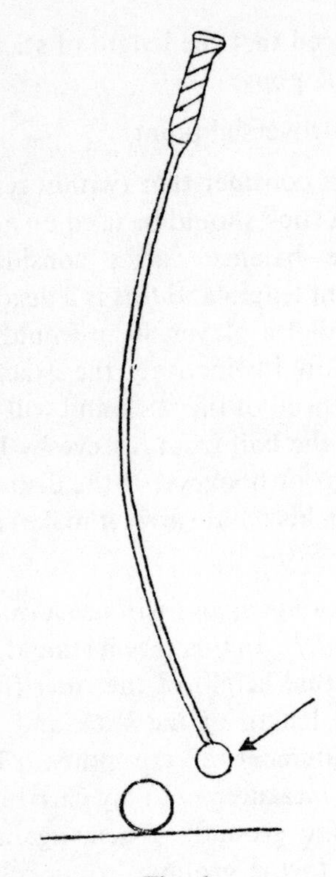

Fig. 1

upper part of the handle, thus tending to strike downwards on top of the ball (*see* Fig. 1). The player who uses a whippy stick learns to compensate instinctively for this disadvantage and times his shot differently to one who, using a stiff cane, has not to allow for it.

Indian players often use very whippy sticks and many

of them are accurate and long hitters; but for Europeans the stiff stick is recommended. It has the advantage of less variability in whippiness whatever may be the wind resistance or the force with which the shot is made; but they cause more strain to the wrist. For this reason some players, when out of practice, start playing with a medium stick and work up to a stiff one as the wrist strengthens.

The beginner, until he has developed his own style, is recommended *not* to use a whippy stick.

It is practically impossible to get a dozen sticks of equal whippiness and balance, but when trying a stick a note should be made where it bends most when striking. The ideal place is from two-thirds to three-quarters down the cane from the handle. Some makers produce a spliced stick which gives this result but they are expensive and, at present, not much used.

Few players realize the importance of finding a handle which really suits them; the majority accept the kind generally made by the manufacturers without question. Some men play best with a thick handle but many can only use a thin one. Various types of handles are given in the catalogues of any polo stick maker and the beginner is recommended to try all of them until he finds one which suits him best.

Some men who find that they are off their game and not hitting the ball cleanly change temporarily to sticks with different handles; the difference in feeling and balance often rectifies any bad habit they may have acquired.

Every man has his own fancies regarding the shape of the head of his stick but the cigar shape is that most generally favoured. The heavier the head the greater the driving power but the diameter of the cylinder is of considerable importance.

(*Note:—For forwards* a $7\frac{1}{2}$ *or* 8 *ounce head is suitable, but backs should seldom use one lighter than* $8\frac{1}{2}$ *to* 9 *ounces.*)

A ball driven along the ground will meet with more resistance and travel less distance than one which has been lifted slightly off the ground. In order to lift the ball it is necessary to have the point of impact with the stick head slightly below the equator of the ball.

On a heavy ground on which the ball lies partly buried, it is advisable to use a head with a smaller diameter than on a level ground or one on which the ball is generally teed up on the grass (*see* Figs. 2 and 3).

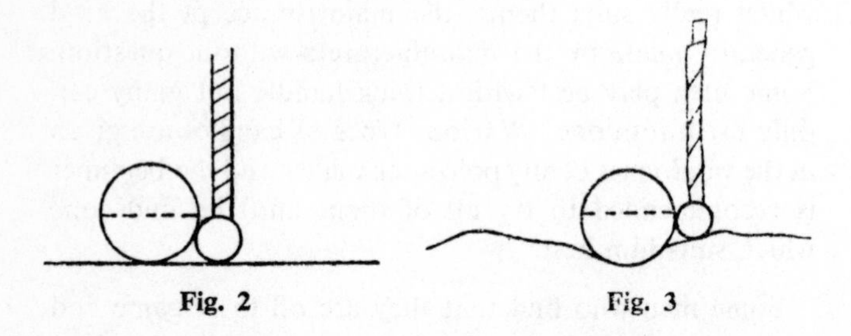

Fig. 2 **Fig. 3**

When a head with less diameter is used its length must be proportionately increased, otherwise, being lighter, it will lose some of its driving power.

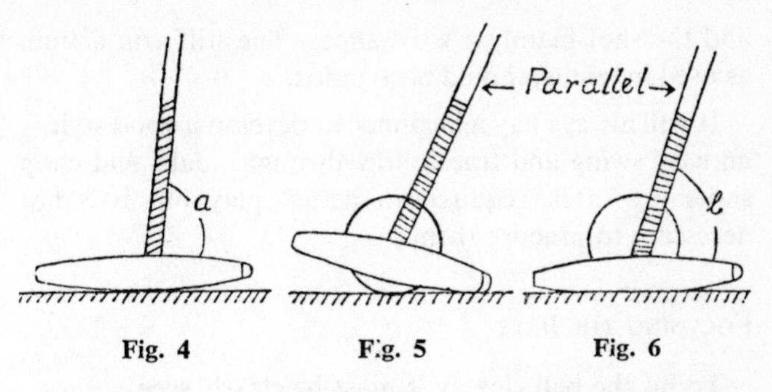

Fig. 4

Angle (*a*) is too nearly a right angle.

Fig. 5

Effect of too perpendicular a junction.

Fig. 6

Angle (*b*) is less than angle (*a*) and position of head more suitable.

Finally, it is as well to decide the angle which the cane and the head are to bear to one another. When making the shot the head of the stick should be parallel to the ground. If the aforesaid angle is nearly a right angle, it will be difficult to hit cleanly a ball which is far from the pony. The majority of shots are made some distance from the pony and the angle needs to be decreased accordingly.

The beginner is recommended to select sticks with an angle of about 70 degrees between the cane and axis of the head.

True Action in Striking

It has been said in Chapter I that at the moment of impact of stick and ball the arm of the striker should be absolutely straight. This does not necessitate a stiff arm or a flail-like action. The arm should be kept flexible and the shot mainly a wrist shot. The stiff arm action, as used in tennis, should be avoided.

It will always pay a beginner to develop a good style—an easy swing and true follow through. Jabs and chop shots are often required in actual play but it is not necessary to practise them.

Focusing the Ball

To hit the ball cleanly it must be clearly seen.

A " good eye " for ball games includes not only perfect and automatic co-operation between hand and eye but also the power to *focus clearly* the ball just before the moment of impact. The latter attribute can be acquired by concentration and practice.

An object vaguely seen will seldom be accurately struck.

In this connection a word of advice and warning is given. In order to focus the ball clearly at the psychological moment, it is not necessary to glare at it fixedly for some time previously! In fact it is undesirable to concentrate on the ball for too long before making a stroke; the eye is merely tired and strained by so doing. Many a player who is away on his own making a run down the field mishits an easy shot because he has concentrated his vision on the ball for too long.

Timing and Clean Hitting

To hit a long ball at polo great strength is not required; the secret lies in accurate timing and clean hitting.

The ball will travel farthest if it can be lifted slightly off the ground and so escape the friction which movement along the surface must create.

A shot is correctly timed when at the moment of impact the head of the stick is moving in the correct direction *and* at its maximum speed.

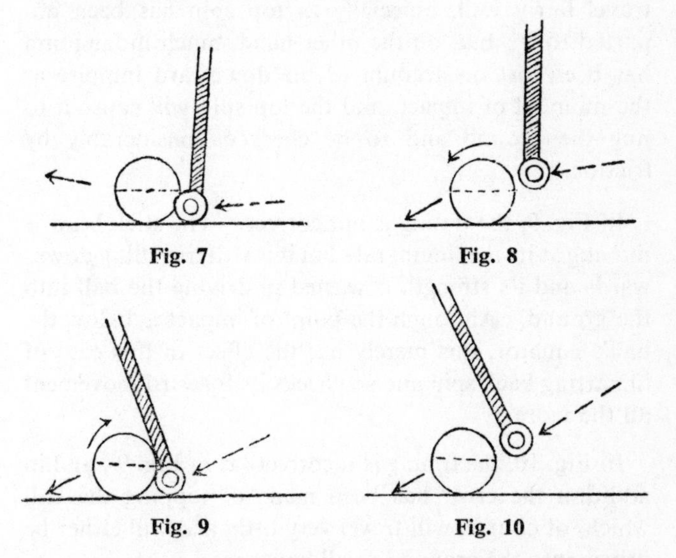

Fig. 7 **Fig. 8**

Fig. 9 **Fig. 10**

In each of the four diagrams given above let us assume that the head of the stick is at the moment moving at its *maximum* speed.

In Fig. 7, the timing is correct. The stick head is at the lowest point of the circle of swing and is about to move in an upward direction. This, combined with the fact that the point of impact is below the equator of the ball, will tend to raise it from the ground. This ball should travel well.

In Fig. 8, the timing is correct. The stick is at the bottom of the circle of swing *but* the point of impact is above the equator of the ball, i.e., the ball has been topped. The timing having been correct the ball will travel fairly well, especially as top spin has been imparted to it; but, on the other hand, much momentum has been lost on account of the downward impulse at the moment of impact, and the top spin will cause it to hug the ground and so be checked considerably by friction.

In Fig. 9, the timing is not correct. The stick head is moving at its maximum rate but it is still travelling downwards and its strength is wasted in driving the ball into the ground. Although the point of impact is below the ball's equator, this merely has the effect in this case of imparting back spin and so checks its forward movement all the more.

In Fig. 10, the timing is incorrect (as in Fig. 9), and in addition the error has been made of topping the ball which, of course, will travel very little and will either be driven into the ground or will bounce.

The Strokes

There are four basic strokes, viz., the forehand and backhand strokes on the off side of the pony and similar strokes on the near side. All other strokes are variations of these.

The strokes on the near side are the more difficult and need the most practice; the ideal being, of course, equal accuracy on both sides.

The grip of the handle is slightly altered for forehand and backhand strokes.

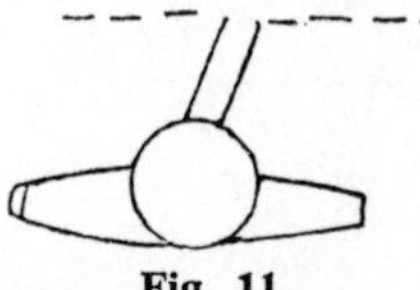

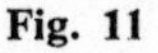

Fig. 11

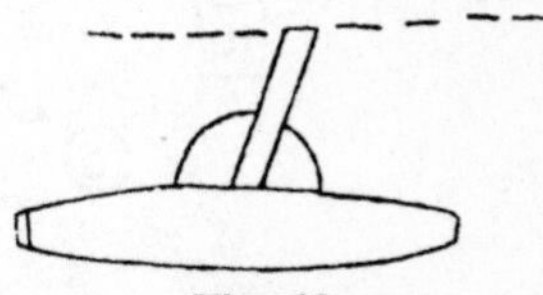

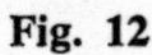

Fig. 12

The grip is as shown in Fig. 11 for { Off side forehanders and Near side backhanders;

and that shown in Fig. 12 is for { Off side backhanders and Near side forehanders

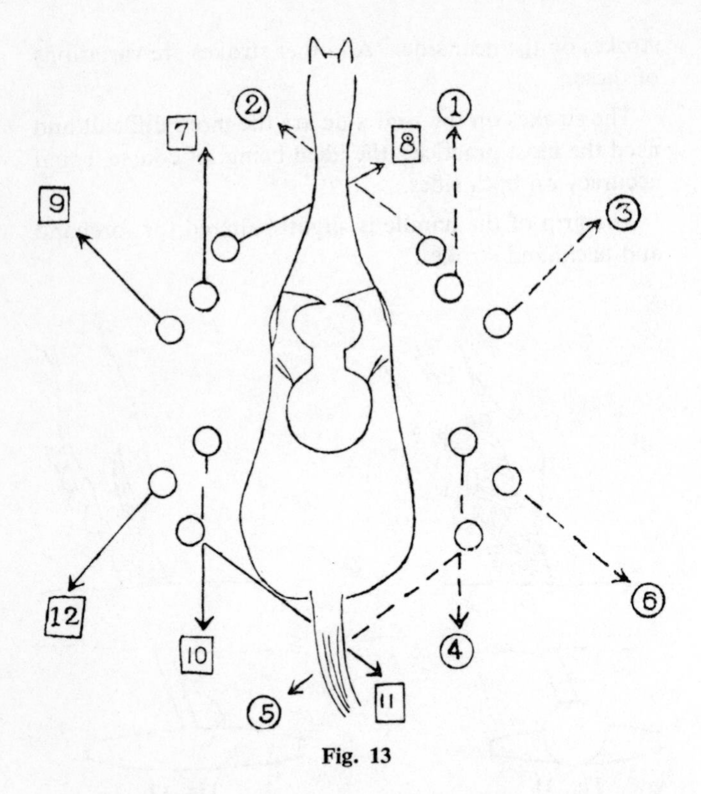

Fig. 13

The two latter shots need the support of the thumb which is placed down the handle as shown.

For all shots struck with the front face of the stick the grip in Fig. 11 is used; and the grip in Fig. 12 is used for all shots struck with the back face of the stick.

For purposes of practice there are twelve strokes which are given in Fig. 13. The approximate position of the ball with reference to the pony at the moment of impact is shown in each case; it will be seen to vary.

" Push out " shots (i.e., 3, 6, 9, and 12) should be taken as far out from the pony as possible. No. 9 is by far the most difficult shot to do.

A moment's thought will show that the pony must not be allowed to gallop up to the ball haphazard but that he must be ridden into such a position as to make the desired shot possible. The good horseman will always have an advantage in this respect, especially in actual play, when the striker will be subject to interference from other players.

Saving the Pony's Mouth

A pony which receives a jab in the mouth whenever the ball is hit will very soon take a dislike to polo and also to practice; moreover he will develop so callous a mouth as to be difficult to manage. The beginner must endeavour to get in the habit of slackening the reins as he makes a shot. This is most difficult to do especially with a hot animal. Hence the desirability of acquiring a quiet pony which does not pull, on which to learn the game.

Practising Definite Strokes

Watch any ordinary player hitting the ball about and it will be seen that 90 per cent. of the shots he makes will be plain forehand drives on the off side!! This is the easiest of all shots and needs the least practice. Because it is easy, requires so little effort, and achieves such satisfying results almost every one falls into the habit of using it too much. The novice is urged to fight against this tendency, for it will delay his progress.

The player would do well first of all to devote equal time to all shots and extra time to those which he finds more difficult. A good way of forcing oneself to do this is to do each shot a specified number of times—say ten.

The beginner will do well to concentrate on shots 1, 4, 7 and 10 until he is fairly proficient; that is until he can, with certainty, hit each shot twenty-five to thirty yards three times running whilst moving at a steady canter. He can then begin to attempt the more difficult ones.

Half an hour spent in definite practices is worth more than three times that amount of time in merely " hitting about."

Pace at which to Practise

The need for accuracy in timing has already been alluded to. To acquire this accuracy the player must learn to know (or feel) instinctively exactly where the head of the stick is. He should, without hesitation or effort, be able to touch any point or mark with the centre of his stick head with the same precision as with the tip of his forefinger. This, in the early stages, requires much concentration—later it will become automatic.

Therefore let the first shot he makes in any practice be at a walk; let him concentrate on hitting the ball cleanly below the equator with *the very centre of the head* of his stick. If he succeeds in lifting the ball slightly off the ground and making a perfect shot, he may assume that his hand and eye are in accord and he can begin his practice.

Should the shot fail—should he stub the ground, top the ball or fail to hit it with the *centre* of the stick head, he should repeat the experiment until he can make this shot perfect because until he can do this it is a waste of time to practise at faster paces. Length of shot is not required; that comes later with the assistance of the pace of the pony. Cleanness of hitting is the first thing for which to try.

There is no doubt that until each shot can be made accurately at a walk it should not be tried at a canter. It may be said here that there is no finer discipline for a pony than to be forced to submit to hitting the ball about at a walk; time so spent is never wasted in so far as the pony is concerned.

As proficiency increases the pace of practice may be increased and, of course, when practising for a tournament only the fastest paces should be used because the enhanced wind resistance affects the timing of the shot.

Solo Practice

The principal disadvantage in practice alone is that the ball generally has come to rest before it is struck, whereas in a game the ball must usually be hit at when in motion.

Then, again, in solo practice there will be more time

in which to prepare for each stroke and there are few distractions. This is satisfactory in the elementary stages but as the beginner becomes more proficient it is desirable to add difficulties. An excellent practice is to use two balls and to keep them both going, hitting one beyond the other whilst varying the strokes and the direction of them.

Practice in hitting a moving ball can, of course, be obtained by dribbling but this only affects a few of the strokes.

As has been emphasized before, it is most desirable that the player should set himself definite practices and not hit about in an hapazard manner.

The following are some simple practices:—

(*a*) Take the ball forward, hitting alternately on the off and on the near side.

(*b*) Take the ball round first on a right handed and then in a left handed circle—first using strokes on the off side only and then on the near side only. The left handed circle when using only near side shots is very difficult, even for good hitters.

(*c*) Hit a forehand off side drive—then an off side backhander—turn—then a near side forehander followed by a near side backhander, and so on.

Such practices can be improvised indefinitely and will be found to be invaluable.

Practise in Pairs

This is far superior to solo practice because it has many of the features of actual polo. It entails the use of judgment and striking the ball when it is in movement. It is, however, a practice which will be usually engaged in only by those who can hit the ball fairly well. Definite exercises can be improvised for pair practice. It is excellent training for ponies, especially young ponies.

In a team preparing for a tournament the adjacent pairs, i.e., Nos. 1 and 2, the No. 3 and back, will gain immense benefit by practising together. The capabilities and mannerisms of the other player can be watched and all of this will tend to a better co-operation in a game.

Accuracy

No. 8 of the rules of polo reads as follows:—

" *The side that scores most goals wins the game.*"

It is of no use for a team to play well and to have the best of the game if it cannot shoot goals. Yet how often this very thing occurs! It would be a good plan if in practice games a side forfeited a quarter of a goal for each time it hit the ball behind the opposing back line except through the goal.

To improve accuracy in goal hitting a course, made with small flags irregularly on a ground, may be used. Players are then sent round the course with one or two balls and the time taken to complete the course is noted. The course can be made as difficult as desired by reducing the width of the goals or by limiting the strokes to be used to, say, near side shots only.

Accuracy can only be acquired by definite practices which tie the player down not only to direction but also to distance. Few players reach the standard of great accuracy in the distance to which they can hit the ball.

The Wooden Horse

In the opinion of the writer the wooden horse is of no value except to strengthen the wrist and for a beginner to learn the strokes, and to save his pony's legs while he acquires control of the stick.

Chapter III

THE INDIVIDUAL PLAYER AND HIS ROLE

Forwards

No. 1

IF the captain of a team were asked what attributes he wants in a No. 1, he would probably reply: "Quickness to seize opportunities, power to mark his man, and deadly accuracy in front of goal."

These, of course, are attributes required in all polo players whatever their positions but they apply particularly to No. 1.

To them might be added " Unselfishness." In no position can one have a more thankless task and more need for self-denial.

The writer has on occasions played No. 1 in front of backs who would not or who could not send the ball up and make for him the desired opportunities. For whole chukkers at a time he was tempted to leave his place and go back and fetch the ball himself and so have *some* fun—anything in fact to break the monotony of stopping, turning, riding off the back, stopping, turning again and so on and so on.

Sometimes, in a tournament, he has seen his backs completely outplayed by the opposing forwards and has given way to the temptation to go back and help. With what result? The result that although the opposing forwards were for the moment subdued, the opposing back was left free to attack and score goals, opportunities of which he did not fail to take advantage.

The fact is that the duties of No. 1 are clear and easily understandable. Being, like the back, on the outside edge of the game his task is simplified and he has not, like No. 2 or No. 3, continually to choose between two courses of action. It is not claimed that No. 1 is an easy position in which to play. On the contrary, it is a position most difficult to fill well and it is a remarkable fact that among first class polo players although there are many good Nos. 2, 3 or back there are but few really good No. 1s.

When a player has achieved some degree of skill he plays 2, 3, or back and his place at No. 1 is filled by a novice.

In tournament polo success will very often depend on No. 1. He is second only to No. 2 in importance in the matter of scoring goals, and after all it is the number of goals scored which counts. In club polo the shooting of goals is unimportant and the better players very naturally take the more responsible positions of 2, 3 or back leaving No. 1 for the beginner or, perhaps, weakest hitter in the team.

Duties of No. 1

The duties of No. 1 may be put shortly as follows:—

In defence . . . . (that is when the opponents are in possession of the ball).

To ride off the opposing back and prevent him having an uninterrupted hit at the ball. Mention of " riding off " and hooking sticks has been made already in Chapter I. It will often so happen that No. 1 finds himself at the moment far from his opposing back. He should then " ride off " the nearest opponent.

As a rule he should avoid coming right back into the game because by so doing he will find himself out of position for attack which may develop at any moment. Nevertheless, having (in defence) commenced to ride off a man he should not leave him until he ceases to be dangerous, which normally will be when the opponent's attack has died away.

In attack . . . . he has two courses open to him:—

(1) To give the opposing back the slip and await a pass; or

(2) To ride the opposing back away from his goal mouth and so leave it open for the No. 2 to score.

The former should be the alternative generally adopted, especially if the attack starts at a distance from the opposing goal. Many players will disagree with this view and prefer that No. 1 should make a habit of marking closely the opposing back under all circumstances. This is asking a lot of a player in club polo who plays the game for enjoyment; uninterrupted riding off ceases to be enjoyable after a time.

The duty of forwards is to attack and shoot goals and No. 1 must take his full share in this task. If the No. 1 has the knack of seizing opportunities (i. e., has polo sense) he will give the opposing back the slip and will throw upon the latter the task of marking *him*. Therefore let No. 1 always remember that immediately the defence turns in to attack, his responsibility for marking the opposing back ceases and he should think only of attack UNLESS he is ordered to " ride the man."

It will often occur that when he has succeeded in getting ahead of the back those behind will fail to hit the ball up to him and the enemy back, being free, will be able to make a saving shot. This risk must be taken. The attack is more important than the defence.

The young player at No. 1 will often be faced with the difficulty that the opposing back whom he has been expressly told to mark continuously leaves his correct place and cruises about all over the ground. If No. 1 sticks to him he will almost certainly be admonished for being out of his place. Should he, on the other hand, leave the back allowing him to go free he will find that uncomplimentary remarks about marking his man will be hurled at him. What, then, should he do?

The above peculiar behaviour on the part of a back is a common device employed by an old player who finds himself *too well marked!!* Quietly giving the warning to his No. 3 (who will then take his place) he will attempt to bewilder the opposing No. 2 and upset the tactics of the other team.

The advice to No. 1 is therefore as follows:—

In polo, attack is more important than defence, therefore be more careful to be in position for the attack.

If No. 1 is "riding off" *someone* (not necessarily the back), he is pulling his weight. If the opposing back chooses to move up and play in his No. 2's position, it falls to the opposing No. 3 to deal with him and this he should do if someone else is looking after his usual opponent.

In the course of a game it will often happen that No. 1 and No. 2 change positions. There should be a perfect understanding between them on this matter; No. 1 should, for the time being, undertake the role of No. 2. He will, of course, get into his own place as soon as the situation allows and he should certainly not adopt the attitude "This is No. 2's job and he should be here."

Forwards

No. 2

Everything that has been said of No. 1 applies to No. 2 but on the latter to a far greater extent will depend the result of the game. He it is who must be absolutely accurate in shooting at goal and he will be the driving force in the attack. The success or failure of an attack will generally depend on him.

Choosing the Form of Attack

Assuming that the backs have sent the ball up and so

initiated an attack, the No. 2 will have to decide whether to take the ball through himself or pass it on to No. 1. The position of No. 1 at the moment will generally decide this for, if he is not in a suitable place, it is obviously futile to send the ball up for the enemy back to take.

A useful rough working rule to guide No. 2 in making his decision is that if he is in his own half of the ground it is best to pass the ball up to No. 1. If he is within, say, two easy strokes of the enemy goal, it will generally be better to tell No. 1 to ride the man and to keep control of the ball himself.

It will often occur that matters are not so easy as above depicted. It may be that No. 2 is well marked and doubts whether he will be able to get a second hit at the ball. This would be an occasion for him to hit to No. 1 at all costs and here comes the necessity for accuracy. He must hit the ball to such a position that his No. 1 has a reasonable chance of getting to it before the opposing back.

No. 2 must be a quick thinker. It is most exasperating to the backs to find that their well hit backhanders or drives have not been taken up by their forwards. So No. 2, foreseeing the trend of events, quickly places himself where it is most convenient for the backs to send the ball. He will endeavour to be in a place which gives the back an easy shot rather than a difficult one.

It is important that No. 2 should have an idea of the hitting powers of his backs. It is obviously useless for him to place himself at a distance to which they cannot hit, or so far ahead that he must pull his pony up to a standstill to await the ball. This needs much judgment because the distance will vary with different backs and also from day to day with the same backs.

No. 2—Marking His Man

The opposing No. 3 is the particular enemy of No. 2 and in defence he should do all he can to hinder him. This task is even more important than in the case of No. 1 because the opposing No. 3 will continually come well up into the game and be within easy shooting distance of the goal. Nevertheless it generally so happens that No. 3 is the least well marked man on a side because his opposite number (No. 2) is rightly more concerned with offensive tactics than defence.

The Backs

No. 3

No. 3 is the pivot of the team and the hardest worked man in it. It is not an old man's place. He shares with the back full responsibility for the defence and also must, like a halfback in hockey, be up and taking active parts in all attacks. It is a most suitable place for the captain of a team.

His main object is by long hitting to send the ball up beyond No. 1; he should not be satisfied with a shot which can reach only No. 2, although, of course, it will frequently be unsuitable to pass the ball to No. 1.

To No. 3 and back will fall the responsibility of initiating all attacks and this they can do with long backhanders. They should in any case avoid that distressful habit of dribbling the ball in a circle with a view to a personal run down the ground.

The backs must feed their forwards and not themselves attack.

In club polo it will often be found that the player with some skill is placed at No. 3. Finding that the forwards are poor performers with their sticks, he may begin to play a selfish game and will take the ball through to score goals himself. This is much to be deprecated. It is bad tactics—bad polo.

It is not possible to show in a book of this kind how No. 3 may create opportunities for his forwards. Experience and a suitable temperament are required, coupled with energy and dash. A lazy No. 3 is valueless.

In defence the opposing No. 2 is his special portion; but more is required of him than merely to mark his man. He must, at the same time, be ready to initiate an attack. The back may succeed in making only a weak defensive shot and it is then the duty of No. 3 to help it on.

In attack he will not hesitate to go right up into the game if by so doing he makes a chance of scoring.

The Backs

No. 4 or Back

The quality most looked for in a back is reliability. He must be a safe hitter, the longer the better. His backhanders are his most important shots and a player who is uncertain in them or cannot get length in them should not, in a tournament, be selected to play back.

So long as he is a good hitter it is not of much importance that he should have experience or dash. It is the easiest position in the field but as it is also the most responsible it is customary to place old and experienced players there.

The principal duty of the back is to pass the ball up to No. 2 and all his shots, offensive or defensive, should have this object in view.

No general advice can here be given him as to how to deal with an efficient opposing No. 1 but if he is being troubled by the " limpet " class of opponent he will do well to " ride off " the opposing No. 2 and thus draw on to himself two of his opponents, with obviously satisfactory results for the remainder of his side.

Chapter IV

THE TEAM AND TEAM TACTICS

A POLO team consists of the Forwards (Nos. 1 and 2) and the Backs (No. 3 and the back), but whereas in hockey and association football it is unusual, and even wrong, for backs and halfbacks to move up into the forward line, in polo the four players will often interchange places for a few moments according to the requirements of the situation. This interchange of places does not in any way alter the roles of the forwards and the backs, because one of the latter, if playing up in the place of a forward, should act as a forward for the time being.

The duty of the forwards when on the offensive is to attack and shoot goals; and when on the defensive to obstruct and hinder the opposing backs.

The duty of the backs is to create opportunities for their forwards by sending the ball up beyond them; to support them in the attack; and by long hitting to turn the defence into attack.

As a rough rule it may be said that the No. 3 should

Dangerous use of the stick!

“ Hi! Hi! Don’t cross ”—“ Rot! You were only cantering.”
(A matter of opinion)

aim at hitting the ball up to and beyond No. 1, and the back should attempt to do the same for No. 2.

A purely defensive game is ineffectual and is contrary to the nature of polo. The only defence lies in unceasing attack, and this attack in a well drilled team can be initiated from any part of the ground, at any time, by a single shot.

It is of great importance that a player should be able to realize quickly and clearly whether his side is at any given moment attacking or defending because on this will depend his tactics.

The Defensive

A team may be described as on the defensive when the opposing side is in possession of the ball and is moving forward with it. It should not be assumed that because an opposing back is about to hit, or has just hit, a back-hander, the defensive has begun; on the contrary, so long as the ball so hit (*see* page 67) can be met or otherwise struck by the attacker, the defensive has *not* begun.

Immediately the defensive is forced on a team each member of it should have two objects in mind:—

(1) To prevent one member of the opposing team from hitting the ball.

(2) To be prepared to turn to the attack at any moment.

The first, which is the primary object, is achieved by riding off the nearest opponent, and this should be done at once.

To turn the defence into attack successfully requires polo sense (i.e., the sense of anticipation) superior to the opposing side, for it is necessary to turn in the required direction sooner than they. Of course, if the shot which was to initiate the offensive miscarries, there is the fear that the enemy may be left free to consummate their attack. This risk will often have to be taken.

As has been indicated in Chapter I, the back will generally hit a backhander, if the ball is in the vicinity of his goal mouth, in the direction of the wing. The other members of a good team will turn outwards in that direction and will at once develop an attack up that side of the ground. Actually, this is difficult to do; but so long as the whole team realize the result to be achieved there will be a combined effort which is the best augury of success. The importance of quickness in turning the defence into attack cannot be overestimated; because success in this particular leads to the gain of moral superiority which is so necessary in all games.

The Attack

The attack commences when the team has turned up in the direction of the adversary's goal and is in possession of the ball.

It can be carried out in several ways, the most usual one being to send the ball up ahead of the No. 1 for him to shoot the goal.

Another way is for No. 2 to retain possession, leaving No. 1 to clear the enemy back from the goal mouth.

These may be regarded as the usual straightforward methods. Occasionally it may be found advantageous (or perhaps unavoidable) for the forwards to take the ball out to the side of the ground and then to centre it to the backs who, coming up, can carry it through the goal. In such cases the forwards, having centred the ball, should at once gallop back into the backs' position so as to relieve them of the responsibility of defence.

Advantage lies in carrying the attack up the right hand side of the ground rather than up the left. By moving up the right wing the striker will get his shot at goal from the off or easier side under his pony's neck, and the opposing backs in saving with a backhander will be forced, if they would avoid hitting across their own goal mouth, to use the push-out backhander which is the more difficult to do.

Some teams are so convinced of the advantage of the right wing offensive that they will develop it in preference to an attack straight up the centre of the ground.

The disadvantages of the left wing attack, unless the forwards are strong hitters on the near side of the pony, are obvious.

Passing Up

It is remarkable how few players, when hitting the ball up, take the trouble to hit it up on the correct side of the person to whom they are passing. It would seem that their only object is to hit as long a ball as possible irrespective of the tactical requirements of the game at the moment. This surely shows a very rudimentary knowledge of polo and relegates it to the level of a slogging match.

If accused of this shortcoming, the average player will reply: " It takes me all my time to hit the ball at all; how can I think about direction and strength? "

In this he makes a great mistake. If he will think of the direction and distance to which he wishes the ball to go he will find that his hand and eye, far from being hindered by such additional considerations, will gain in accuracy and will answer in a manner which will surprise him.

Every player should understand where he should hit the ball when passing up to the man in front.

If the latter is free the ball is best passed up on his right side, sufficiently wide (say a yard or so) that it does not hit his pony's legs, and as far ahead of him as possible without reaching any opposing player who may be riding ahead.

If, however, the man to whom the pass is made is being ridden off, the ball should be passed up on his free side and somewhat wide of him so that he can, if necessary, allow himself to be ridden on to it.

The above are two very general rules and are given merely as a guide. No hard and fast rules can be given to cover the multitude of situations which arise in a game.

The necessity is emphasized for the player to make up his mind quickly, exactly where he wishes to place the ball, because no amount of perfection in stick work will be of any avail unless he can do so.

Conversely, the fact of so making up his mind will automatically improve his hitting.

EFFECT OF PERSONAL IDIOSYNCRASIES

The personal idiosyncrasies of players and the abilities of their various ponies have much effect on polo tactics. In a side which practises and plays together continually as a team the peculiarities and weaknesses of each player become known and the tactics of the team are modified accordingly.

For instance, it may be that a player is uncertain in his backhanders. (The team will not turn up to the attack so quickly or so confidently when they see that it is he that is about to hit the ball. They will pause to make sure of the shot.)

Another player may vary considerably from day to day in his hitting. (The team will watch carefully in the first chukker to see whether he is hitting well or not and will not ride so far ahead of him on his bad days as on others when his eye is in.)

Yet another player may be a strong hitter on the off side and be weak on the near side. (The team will be more careful to back him up when he is playing the ball on his near side.)

The number of such instances may be multiplied. Many will regard them as trivial—but it is the sum of such small points which makes a difference in the performance of a team. Consideration of such trifles adds immensely to the interest of the game even in club polo and the man who acquires the habit of noticing the idiosyncrasies of other players will be able to combine with them much better and so improve the polo in his club.

Positions on the Field

In Chapter I it was stated that polo is a fore and aft game and that the positions of the players on the field are only relative to each other. There are, nevertheless, certain generally accepted positions applicable when the ball has gone out of play and is about to be brought into play again. These are:—

Beginning of a chukker.

Throw in from touch.

Penalty hits.

Hitting out from behind.

Beginning of a Chukker

The ball is thrown in at the beginning of a chukker as is depicted in Fig. 14 (page 75) (and in tournaments, after a goal is scored).

In certain teams other positions are adopted; for instance, No. 3 meets the ball in place of No. 1 and whether he hits or misses it, he turns his back towards his own goal in defence leaving the other three players free to attack.

In ordinary club polo, however, it is seldom necessary to depart from the normal positions given in Fig. 14.

Throw In from Touch

Fig. 15 (page 75) shows the normal positions for a throw in from touch.

Penalty Hits

(*a*) *Sixty yards hit.*—The 60 yards hit is given against a side which hits the ball behind its own back line and is taken from a point opposite the place at which the ball crossed the back line.

The normal positions of the attacking side are shown in Fig. 16 (page 76). It will be noticed that the goal mouth is left open.

The defending side places itself where it wishes but not less than 20 yards from the ball.

(*b*) *Forty yards hit.*—This penalty is taken from opposite the centre of the goal. None of the defending side may come out from between the goal posts and may not cross the back line until the ball has been struck.

The positions of the defenders are shown in Fig. 17 (page 76). No. 1 gallops out to meet the ball, followed by No. 2. No. 3 and back, in succession, ride across the goal mouth (*if they can do so without fouling*) and having their stick arms towards the ball may succeed in saving a goal.

Hitting Out from Behind

See Fig. 18. The side hitting out should regard itself as the attacker.

The back hits the ball in such a way that it will not be met by an opposing No. 1 or No. 2. He will then follow it up himself or let No. 3 do so. (This requires previous agreement.) His object is to hit the ball in front of his No. 1 or No. 2, but if the opposing No. 1 and No. 2 are too good for him he may pass it to his No. 3 instead. It may be noted that when hitting out from the left of the goal it is more difficult for him to pass to No. 3 than when hitting out from the right, because the latter requires the easier shot, i.e., under the pony's neck.

In all cases he should so place the ball that the No. 1 or 2 or 3 can take it on at full gallop and not have to pull up for the ball to reach him.

No. 3 protects the goal in the event of the opposing No. 1 or 2 meeting the ball successfully (unless, of course, the back is a sure and long hitter, in which case he might go up further and be prepared to take a pass). Unless he has agreed with the back to remain behind and take his place, he should follow up the forwards and back them up.

No. 2 gets into position on the flank, normally, just behind the 25 yards line and about half-way between the goal and the touch line. He will begin to canter forward as the back canters up to hit the ball and should get on to the line of the ball *without crossing* and take it on at full gallop. The actual distance from the back line that the No. 2 takes his position depends on the hitting powers of the back. He should not go up so far as to necessitate waiting at a standstill for the ball to reach him.

No. 1 should remember that his side is attacking and that at the moment he is not required to mark his man. He should place himself in such a position that a long hit out from the back can pass ahead of him and so that he can take it on. He can also often prevent the opposing No. 3 meeting the ball by hooking his stick. If his No. 2 gets the ball, the No. 1 may either gallop ahead to await a pass or move over to ride the enemy back clear of the goal mouth. He will do whichever seems most advantageous at the time.

Meeting a Hit Out from Behind

See Fig. 18. The positions recommended are given in this figure. The side may consider itself as attacking—for it will not be possible to mark properly the opposing numbers.

The Nos. 1 and 2 gallop to their places about 10 yards from the 25 yards line and get into position more or less level with each other, from 15 to 20 yards apart, and facing the ball. As the opposing back is about to hit the ball they should begin to move forward; they should not await the ball at a standstill. Their object is, of course, to meet the ball *without crossing the line of it.*

No. 3 goes to a position near the touch line about 20 to 30 yards behind No. 2 and will face the ball with the intention of meeting it should No. 2 fail to do so.

The back will remain in the centre of the ground on the defensive and paying particular attention to the opposing No. 3 (to whom the ball may be sent).

Chapter V

FOULING

A PLAYER of club polo once remarked that, in his club, quite half the game consisted in fouling, and this occasioned more excitement than the game itself.

It is a remarkable fact that in polo, the most dangerous of all games, *one seldom has umpires*, except, of course, in tournaments. Still more remarkable is it that in polo fouling is regarded by many with a lenient eye, perhaps as exhibiting an enterprising spirit or as an indication of pluck!

Let it here be stated quite definitely that, in the opinion of the writer, deliberate fouling is a practice beneath contempt; a practice contrary to all the principles of fair play and one which is not tolerated in any other game. Yet in polo we find men with a superior knowledge of the game or better mounted than others, deliberately fouling in order to gain an advantage.

The writer has heard the opinion expressed that it is

sometimes incumbent on a player *in a tournament* to risk a foul if thereby he benefits his side. Although this point of view is not accepted there is this to be said for it that, in a tournament, men are usually playing among others who know the game and also there are two umpires present whose sole duty is to watch for such fouls. In club games no such excuse exists.

All fouls, except that of wrongly hooking sticks, are dangerous.

By fouling, a player not only risks damage to his opponent but also imperils the ponies of both. In addition to the inhumanity of hurting an animal, a man by fouling risks another man's money, a liberty which not even a game concedes.

Setting aside the contemptible practice of deliberate fouling, players may foul because they are ignorant of the rules; their ponies are out of control; they are excited and lose their heads; or, they are forced into a foul by another player.

Ignorance of the Rules

Unfortunately an academic knowledge of the rules given in the *Polo Calendar* is not sufficient. Most fouls are dependent upon the relative pace of the ponies at the time. Experience and judgment are required to understand a foul thoroughly. In the heat and excitement of a game many men are incapable of judging relative pace and only a trained impartial observer (the umpire) can really decide a foul.

How often one hears the shout " Hi! Hi! Don't cross!!! " and the reply " Rot! It wasn't a cross. You are only cantering."

Ignorance of the rules cannot be condoned but undoubtedly more than an academic knowledge of them is necessary and a beginner must endeavour to recognize fouling by observation of actual play.

Ponies Out of Control

A pony out of control is a danger to life and limb not only of the rider but of all the other players and their ponies. The rules of polo definitely provide that such ponies shall be ordered off the ground. In a tournament they are so ordered and in club polo it is the duty of the polo committee to protect players by doing likewise. Nevertheless, it is true that, ridden by an experienced player, even difficult ponies may be played without danger to others. Bad horsemen who cannot control any pony should, of course, be debarred from playing in fast chukkers until more proficient.

The foul most commonly perpetrated by those on bad ponies is " dangerous riding " (a foul often confused with " crossing " which is quite a different thing. Examples of both are given later).

Excitement and Confusion

It is difficult for a beginner to " sort out the situation " in a confused game and many are incapable of keeping calm in the heat of a chukker. Those who can do so have an immense advantage.

Elsewhere in this book it has been stated that "a man who, owing to his inflexibility in the saddle or for any other reason, can only look to his front will be a danger to his fellow players."

A good player will frequently glance round to note the positions of others, positions which change with kaleidoscopic rapidity. It is obvious that if he omits to do this he will repeatedly run the risk of fouling.

Let the beginner therefore avoid being too engrossed in the pursuit of the ball or man. He should try to keep continually in his mind a picture of the game as it is at the moment. He will find, with experience, that he can foresee the movements of other players and will need only a glance to confirm his anticipations.

Being Forced into a Foul

This is an uncommon foul but it is mentioned because a keen and energetic beginner will sometimes ride his man off successfully and simultaneously force him across the line of the ball or into dangerous riding. It is obvious that a man so ridden off is not fouling. The player who forces him into such a position commits the foul.

Some Common Fouls

The two outstanding fouls in polo are "crossing" and "dangerous riding."

Crossing is a form of dangerous riding but is a form of it which contravenes a special rule of polo and is therefore considered separately.

Many players thoroughly understand the rule about crossing and consider that so long as they do not actually cross they are committing no foul. This is not so; they may none the less be riding dangerously, a foul difficult to define and one which more often than not an umpire only is in a position to judge.

Crossing

Imagine that the polo ball is travelling or has just travelled on a certain line. No player may *cross* that line or that line produced if, in so doing, he interferes with or endangers another player who is moving on that line. The latter is said to be " in possession " of the ball and all other players must give way to him.

It often happens that two men are simultaneously on the line of the ball one of whom is following and the other meeting it. In this case both are " in possession " and neither need give way but both *must* take the shot on the off side otherwise their ponies would meet head to head.

The beginner may ask " If I am to give way to the man in possession of the ball what is to prevent him taking it on through the goal? "

The answer is:—

Hook his stick, or
Ride him off the line, or

Get on to the line ahead of him and so become in possession of the ball, or

Cross the line of the ball so far ahead of him that he and his pony are not endangered.

These two latter proceedings need judgment because in either event if the man in possession is forced to check his pony in the slightest degree he has been fouled. The pace at which he is moving always affects the case but the beginner will do well until experience has given him judgment to assume that the aforesaid player is moving, or is about to move, at his maximum speed.

Some men do not fully understand the meaning of the expression " line of the ball." They assume that if they themselves gallop parallel to the *sides of the ground* they " are on the line." This, of course, is not so. The line of the ball is that line on which it has just travelled, the sides of the ground do not affect the situation.

The hit out from the back line is the most usual occasion for crossing. Both sides are equally inclined to foul at such a time and umpires invariably watch carefully for it. The No. 2 of the side hitting out will generally tend to cross the line of the ball in taking it on and thus foul one of the opposing side who is meeting the ball on the correct line. On the other hand the opposing Nos. 1 and 2 will generally risk cutting in when meeting the ball and thus cross the striker who is (or should be) following it up.

DANGEROUS RIDING

The meaning of this is evident. Many a player will

avoid crossing and yet will foul in this manner.

The following is a common example.

The ball has been struck by the opposing side. The defending back gets on to the line of the ball ahead of the striker who follows him closely (say, a couple of horses' lengths behind). The back then hits a backhander, checks his pony, and begins to turn to that side on which the ball was when he struck at it.

This is a foul—dangerous riding.

The back in so turning has crossed the line on which the ball *was* moving and thereby endangered the previous striker who was following up and who may be moving at a faster pace than he. It is not a cross because the ball has begun to move on a new line when the foul occurs.

The foul of dangerous riding is most often made when a player hits a near side backhander, because many men in making this shot throw their weight over and thus force their ponies across the line of the ball. The beginner (and, in fact, all players of club polo) should make it an invariable rule to turn, after hitting a backhander, *away* from the side on which the ball was when they struck at it.

Zigzagging in front of an opponent is another form of dangerous riding. At a slow pace this cannot, of course, be regarded as a foul but when playing fast it certainly is one.

A trick employed by old hands (a trick which has now been definitely ruled as a foul) is that of riding in at an angle to the line of the ball as though about to cross and then at the last moment, swinging either on to the line or right away from it, or even stopping completely just before reaching it. By so doing he puts the man in possession off his shot, for the latter will generally anticipate a cross or a severe bump and will have his attention taken off the ball.

Another form of dangerous riding, which is very difficult to avoid, is this. A player, better mounted than his opponent, rides off the man he is marking, passes slightly ahead and then pulls his pony, perhaps inadvertently, across the front of him. In fast polo many a bad fall has been occasioned in this manner.

The angle at which ponies may be made to bump into each other varies. On hard slippery grounds where the consistency of the soil or the depth of the turf does not give ponies' feet much purchase (as, for instance, in the East), the angle of bump will seldom safely exceed 40 degrees. In America and England, where the surface of the ground holds better, the angle is often increased without danger of fouling by dangerous riding.

Dangerous Use of the Stick

Every player is entitled to a legitimate shot at the ball but in so doing he must avoid striking with his stick another player or pony.

It must be understood, however, that a player who deliberately rides his pony on to the stick of a man making a backhander does so at his own risk.

For instance, a back is on the line of the ball and is

about to make a backhander on the off side. The opposing No. 1 is also on the line of the ball and is overtaking him. The back in this case is not debarred from making his shot. The No. 1 should change over and meet the ball by a forehand near side shot (*see* illustration on page 67). Should he be foolish enough to ride his pony straight on to the ball and thereby have it struck by the back's stick, he cannot claim a foul.

Shots made under the pony's neck at wide angles will often lead to a foul, especially if whippy sticks are used. For instance, a player is being ridden off by an opponent who is on his near side. He leans forward and makes a shot to the left under his pony's neck and in so doing hits with his stick his opponent's pony. It is a foul—dangerous use of the stick.

To strike at a ball which is a yard or less immediately in front of an opponent's pony is generally a foul. Although it may be only a dribbling shot, which of itself will not damage a pony, yet there is the danger of tripping him.

Some players have a habit of swinging their sticks continuously when galloping after a ball. This becomes a foul if an opponent's pony which is catching up from behind is likely to be struck or frightened by it.

In conclusion it may be said that were it not for fouling there would be little of that bad language and bad feeling which is so common a feature of polo. There is no doubt that few beginners learn the fouls until, playing in a tournament, the umpire penalizes them.

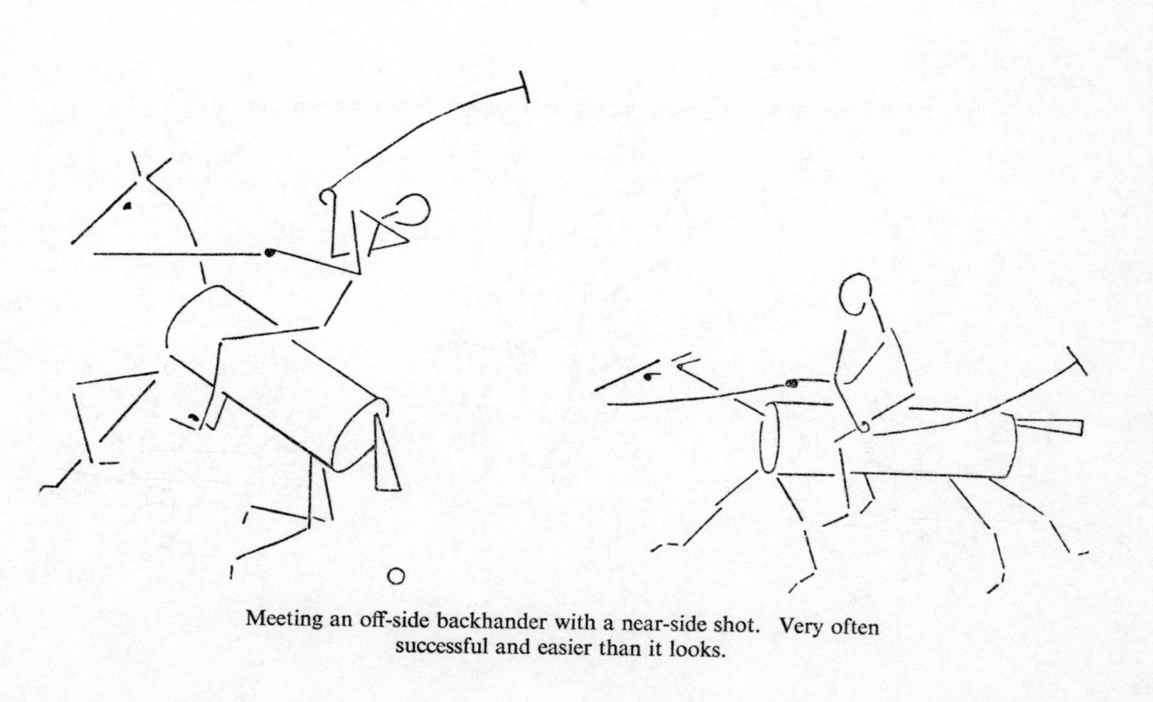

Meeting an off-side backhander with a near-side shot. Very often successful and easier than it looks.

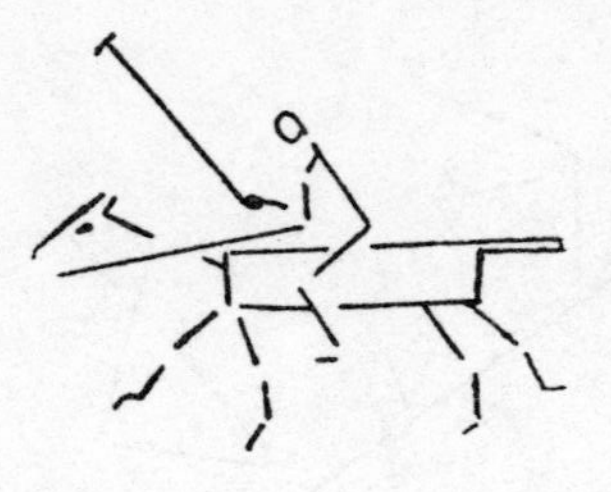
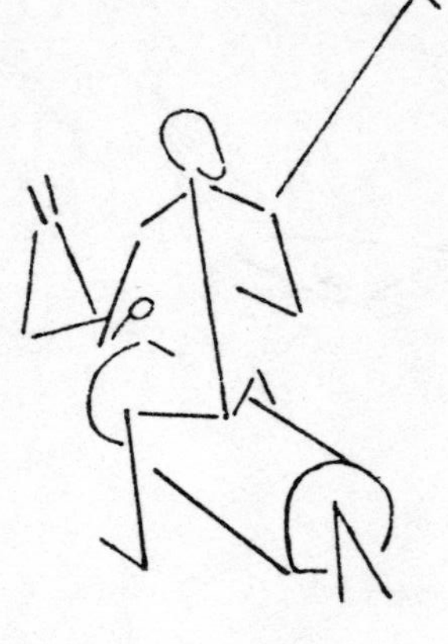
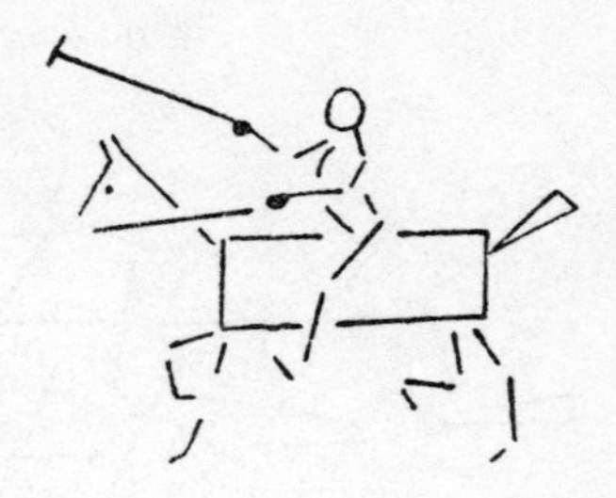

He urges the beginner to ride his man but he himself avoids any hard work.

Chapter VI

CLUB POLO

THERE is the danger, if a game is taken too seriously, that it may become a business; a business which breeds the type (yearly increasing in all games) that may be described as the " amateur professional."

A certain proportion of players of club polo do not belong to any particular team. They play for the sake of the game rather than the prizes it may win. Unfortunately, the interpretation of what constitutes " the game " varies. Many men play entirely for their own amusement, to get as much fun for themselves irrespective of the true game and its tactics. These are the men who ruin club polo which becomes debased by them into a combined slogging match. Above all they are the downfall and despair of beginners!

Often the oldest and most experienced players on the field, they avoid all such unpleasant duties as passing the ball or riding off the man, and leaving their correct positions they play for their own hand. Beginners modelling themselves on these experts soon give up any attempt to play on sound lines.

Let the beginner take heart. If his eyes are opened to the malevolent habits of these old hands, he can observe and yet *not* imitate them; thus will he retain the power to improve his own game which otherwise he might lose.

How to Improve the Standard

At the risk of the disillusionment of the tiro let it be whispered that much of this incorrect play by experienced players is due, not to selfishness at all but, alas, to ignorance.

A strange peculiarity of polo is that a man may play it for years and yet remain ignorant of the elementary principles.

One of the features of club polo which tends to arrest improvement is that a player not only incessantly changes his partners in play but also changes his position in the side. This, of course, by providing variety, adds to the interest of the game; none the less it leads to confusion of thought.

In some places attempts to combat this disadvantage are made by arranging small tournaments either on the "Ladder" or "American" system. Anything in the nature of a tournament or competition necessitates pressing ponies to their utmost and many men, for obvious reasons, are unwilling to do this continually.

A good solution to all these difficulties appears to be as

follows. Let each polo club make sure that every playing member really understands the principles of the game and has a clear idea as to the duties of each player in a team. This could be done in many ways but perhaps the easiest would be to have printed some polo notes or club rules, a copy of which each player would receive and to which he would be requested to conform. Such a procedure would certainly dispel ignorance and might (who knows!) even shame the selfish player into a less egotistical method of play.

Help the Beginner

A plea for the better encouragement of the beginner may well find place here.

The beginner is invariably requested to play No. 1. At his anxious and devoted head is much instruction flung, and abuse! Confused and upset by the movement and wind, he can hear little and understand less; most of the time his back is to the game and he sees very little of what is going on.

The easiest place on the field is back; at back one sees most of the game. It is here, then, that the beginner, seeing most, will learn most. In club polo it matters little whether a side wins or loses and the weak hitting of an inexperienced back is of no great importance. It is urged that in at least one chukker in four a beginner should be made to play back. The confidence and experience gained are out of all proportion to the sacrifice made by the other players. Moreover, if the opposing

No. 1 is also a beginner, two evenly matched players are thus set to mark each other.

SHOUTING ON THE POLO FIELD

Few people when playing hear anything that is shouted to them on the polo field, and it is generally a waste of time to give directions during play. In some good teams, orders on the field have been reduced to two, i.e., the words " Go " (meaning, leave the ball to me) and " Turn." Many beginners are much discouraged by being shouted at and cases have been known of young players even giving up polo on this account. " Why should I play polo to be abused " is the thought engendered—for it is unhappily true that instructions during play more often than not take the form of abuse.

The beginner is recommended to approach, after the game, any older player who has shouted at him and ask what he was doing wrong and explain, if necessary, that he regrets that he cannot hear instructions during play. It is a fact that most players in the excitement and heat of a game say things that they not only do not mean to be offensive but which they also have after the game completely forgotten.

CONCLUSION

In these pages an attempt has been made to give a simple explanation of, and some hints on, polo. It is not claimed that all the ground has been covered; for that, a large volume would be required.

On many controversial points a definite opinion has been given because the beginner (for whom this book has principally been written) desires above all things a definite ruling; anything, in fact, to clear up the confusion which polo invariably creates in his mind. Later on, experience will show him that polo cannot be governed by rules to cover all situations.

When in doubt how to act, let him do as he would in a tournament playing with and against first class players.

DON'T—

1. Hit the ball across your own goal mouth.
2. Ride through the enemy's goal mouth.
3. Ride level with one of your own side.
4. Stand over the ball.
5. Follow up too closely.
6. Hit the ball towards the wing except near your own goal.
7. Use whippy sticks.
8. Practise hitting about haphazardly.
9. Be satisfied with a low standard of accuracy.
10. Leave the ball unless told to do so.

Do—

1. Learn the duties of each position before playing.
2. Learn the rules.
3. Keep your eye on the *game*.
4. Mark someone when defending.
5. Ride close to the man you are marking.
6. Hook sticks whenever possible.
7. Back up your own man.
8. Remember attack is more important than defence.
9. Be unselfish.
10. Play for the team.

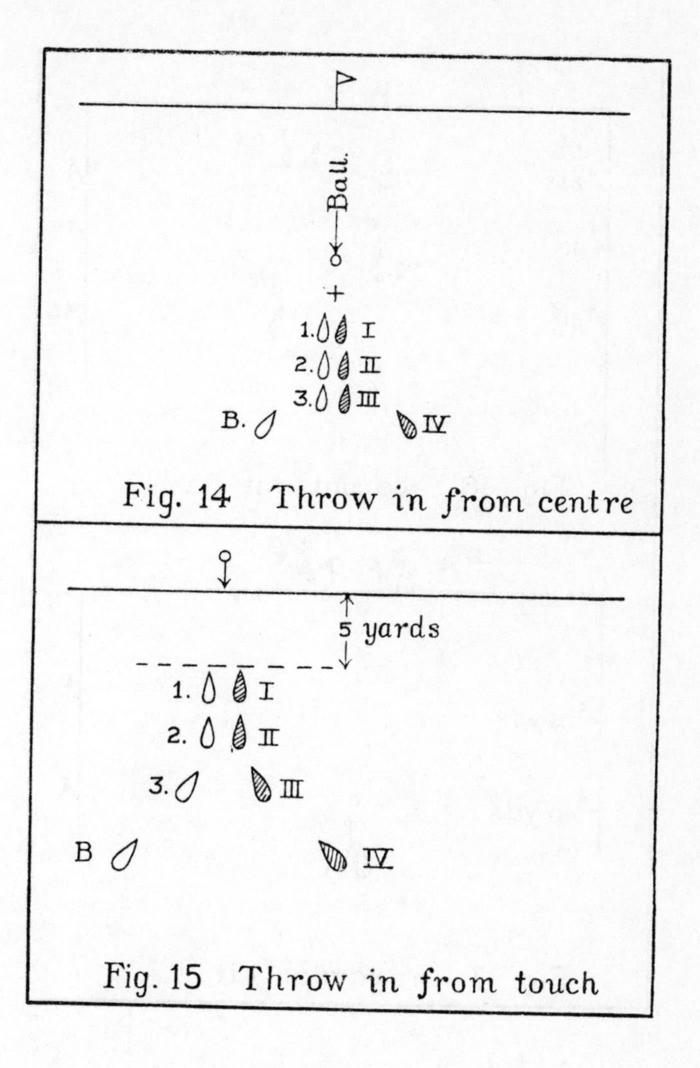

Fig. 14 Throw in from centre

Fig. 15 Throw in from touch

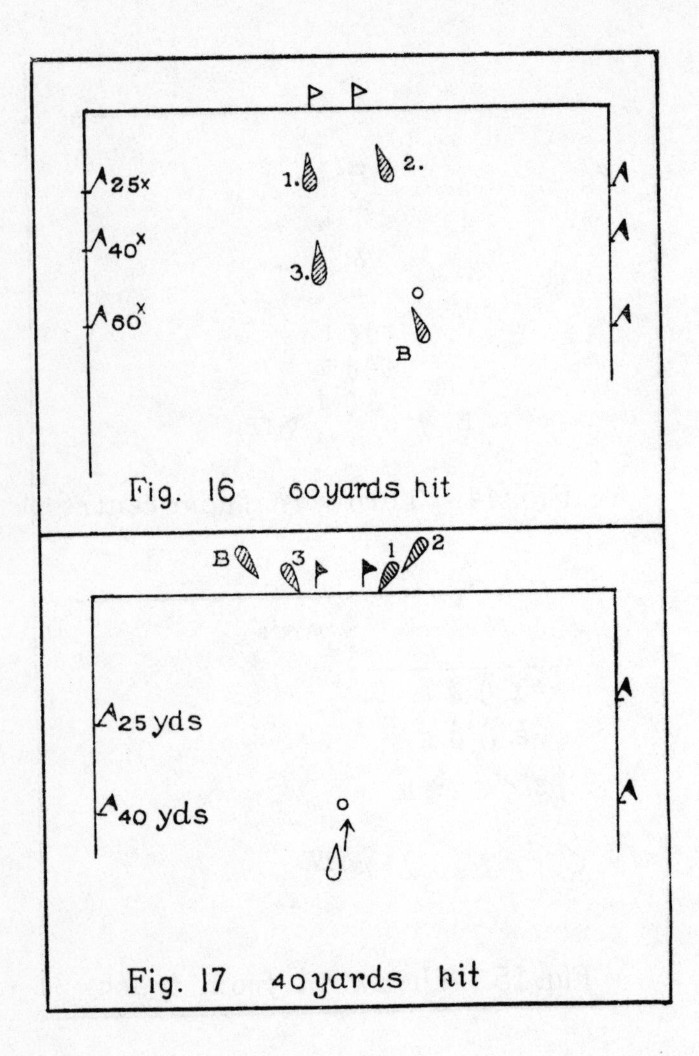

Fig. 16 60 yards hit

Fig. 17 40 yards hit

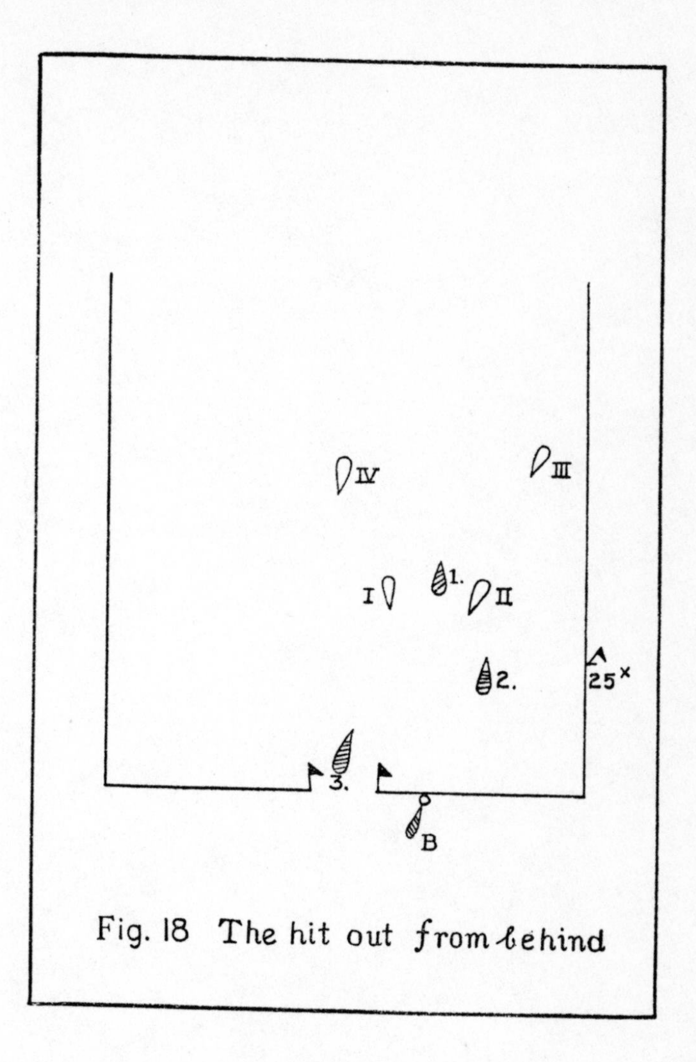

Fig. 18 The hit out from behind